Indiana

by **Ed Pell**

Consultant:
Sheryl Vanderstel
Independent History
Education Consultant

Capstone
press
Mankato, Minnesota

Capstone Press
151 Good Counsel Drive • P.O. Box 669 • Mankato, Minnesota 56002
http://www.capstone-press.com

Library of Congress Cataloging-in-Publication Data
Pell, Ed.
   Indiana / by Ed Pell.
   v. cm.—(Land of liberty)
   Includes bibliographical references and index.
   Contents: About Indiana—The land, climate, and wildlife—History of Indiana—
Government and politics—Economy and resources—People and culture.
   ISBN 0-7368-1582-1 (hardcover)
   1. Indiana—Juvenile literature. [1. Indiana.] I. Title. II. Series.
F526.3 .P45 2003
977.2—dc21

                                             2002011781

Summary: An introduction to the geography, history, government, politics, economy,
resources, people, and culture of Indiana, including maps, charts, and a recipe.

Editorial Credits
Amanda Doering, editor; Jennifer Schonborn, series designer; Linda Clavel, book designer;
   Angi Gahler, illustrator; Karrey Tweten, photo researcher; Eric Kudalis, product
   planning editor

Photo Credits
Cover images: McAllister's covered bridge, James P. Rowan; Indy cars, Index Stock
   Images/Randy Lorenzen

AP/Wide World Photos, 46; Bill Johnson, 56; Capstone Press/Gary Sundermeyer, 54;
Corbis, 4; Corbis/Bettmann, 31, 44; Corbis/Layne Kennedy, 50–51; Folio Inc., 45;
Hulton Archive by Getty Images, 22, 38; Index Stock Images/David Davis, 63;
Indiana Tourism Division, 25, 26, 32–33, 48, 52, 53; James P. Rowan, 10, 12–13, 16, 40;
North Wind Picture Archives, 19, 21, 23, 29, 58; One Mile Up, Inc., 55 (top and bottom);
Panoramic Images/ImageState/P. Hopkins, 42–43; Paramount Press/Robert Griffing, 24;
PhotoDisc, Inc., 1, 14, 57; Stock Montage, Inc., 27; Unicorn Stock Photos, 8, 34;
USFWS/Andy King, 15; U.S. Postal Service, 59

Artistic Effects
PhotoDisc, Inc.

1 2 3 4 5 6 08 07 06 05 04 03

Table of Contents

Chapter 1 About Indiana 5

Chapter 2 Land, Climate, and Wildlife 9

Chapter 3 History of Indiana 17

Chapter 4 Government and Politics 35

Chapter 5 Economy and Resources 41

Chapter 6 People and Culture 47

Maps Indiana's Cities .7
Indiana's Land Features 11

Features Recipe: Honey Baked Apples 54
Indiana's Flag and Seal 55
Almanac 56
Timeline 58
Words to Know 60
To Learn More .61
Internet Sites .61
Places to Write and Visit 62
Index 64

Fans crowd the stands to watch a race at the Indianapolis Motor Speedway.

Chapter 1

About Indiana

At the Indianapolis 500, racecar engines roar and hum. The fans in the stands cheer for their favorite drivers. The announcer calls out, "Gentlemen, start your engines." This call has begun almost every Indy 500 race at the Indianapolis Motor Speedway since 1911. The Indy 500 is the world's most famous car race.

The race is run at Indianapolis Motor Speedway's 2.5-mile (4-kilometer) track. The Indy 500 is held on Memorial Day weekend. About 400,000 people attend the event. Millions of TV viewers watch around the world.

In 1909, the first 500-mile (805-kilometer) race was run. Ray Harroun won that race with an average speed of 74 miles

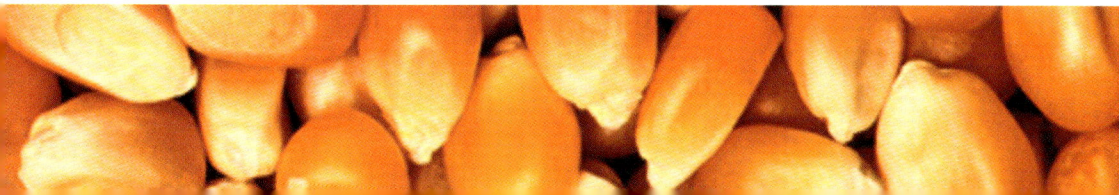

(119 kilometers) per hour. Today, winners average well over 200 miles (322 kilometers) per hour.

The Hoosier State

Indiana is known as the Hoosier State. People from Indiana are called Hoosiers, but no one knows exactly why. Some people think the nickname goes back to a Kentucky man named Sam Hoosier. Hoosier only hired people from Indiana. Another reason is found in Indiana folktales. When visitors knocked on cabin doors in Indiana, they were greeted with the question, "Who's 'ere?" Indiana natives said it so fast it sounded like "Hoosier."

Another nickname for Indiana is the Crossroads of America. Indiana is called the crossroads because it is in the middle of the country. Many interstate highways also cross in Indiana.

Indiana is the smallest of the Midwestern states. Lake Michigan borders Indiana to the northwest. Michigan is to the north, and Ohio is to the east. Kentucky lies to the south. Illinois is to the west.

Indiana's Cities

Lake Michigan

M I C H I G A N

● South Bend

● Gary

Fort Wayne ●

Wabash River

● Kokomo

● Lafayette

I N D I A N A

● Muncie

O H I O

Indianapolis ✪

● Terre Haute

Bloomington ●

● Columbus

I L L I N O I S

Ohio River

● Evansville

K E N T U C K Y

N
W   E
S

Legend

✪ Capital

● City

〜 River

Scale
Miles
0   20   40   60   80

0   20 40 60 80 100
Kilometers

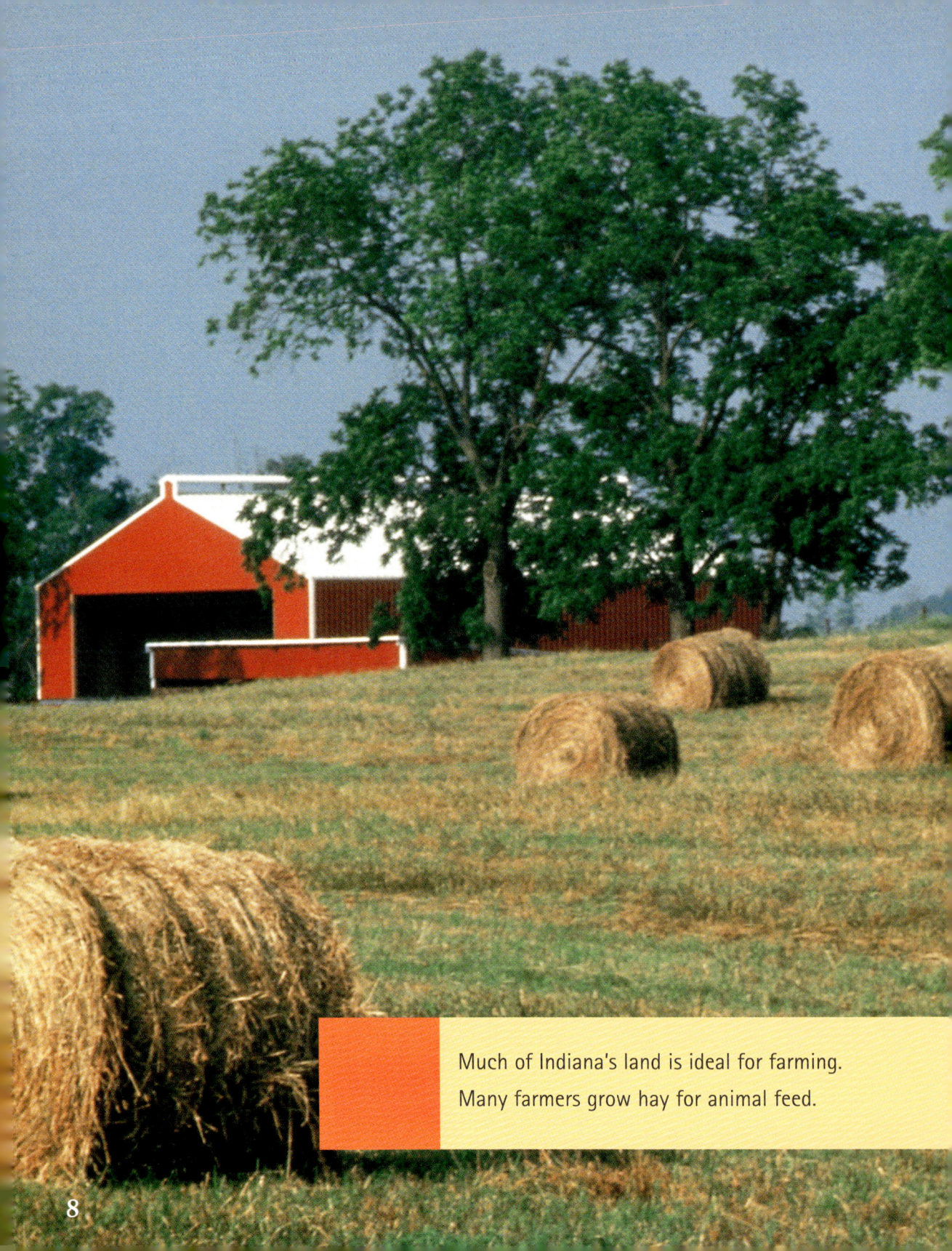

Much of Indiana's land is ideal for farming.
Many farmers grow hay for animal feed.

Chapter 2

Land, Climate, and Wildlife

Indiana is part of the Interior Plains. The Interior Plains spread from the Canadian border through the center of the United States. Most of Indiana lies between 500 and 1,000 feet (152 and 305 meters) above sea level.

Land

The Central Lowland covers northern and central parts of the state. Sheets of ice called glaciers flattened the land. They left behind soil made of sand, clay, and gravel. This soil is good for farming.

Unlike the lowlands, southern Indiana is very hilly. Many caves can be found in southern Indiana. Wyandotte Cave is a popular tourist spot. The cave contains the Pillar of the Constitution, a huge rock formation.

About 200 years ago, 85 percent of Indiana was covered by forests. By 1860, more than half of the state's forests had been cut down. Settlers considered forestland the best land for farming.

Today, less than 20 percent of Indiana is covered with forests. Indiana's trees include dogwoods, sycamores, oaks, pines, and maples. Some farmers are now replacing crops with hardwood trees. Hardwood trees can be made into furniture.

Turkey Run State Park in west-central Indiana is covered in forests. Some of the trees are old growth trees, meaning they were not planted by anyone.

Indiana's Land Features

Lake Michigan

Tippecanoe River

Wabash River

Hoosier Hill

White River

Monroe Reservoir

Ohio River

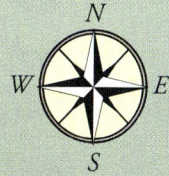

N
W   E
S

Legend

▲ Highest Point

〜 River

Scale
Miles
0   20   40   60   80
0   20   40   60   80   100
Kilometers

Water

Indiana has more than 400 lakes. These lakes include natural ones, such as Lake Wawasee, and artificial ones such as Lake Monroe.

The longest river in Indiana is the Wabash. The river is celebrated in the state song, "On the Banks of the Wabash Far Away." The city of Wabash is named after the Wabash River. Other rivers in Indiana include the Kankakee, Tippecanoe, and White Rivers.

Climate

Indiana has warm summers and cool winters. The average summer temperature is 73 degrees Fahrenheit (23 degrees Celsius). The average winter temperature is 30 degrees Fahrenheit (minus 1 degree Celsius). The first frost of fall usually happens in October.

Northern Indiana averages 36 inches (91 centimeters) of rainfall per year. Southern Indiana averages 44 inches (112 centimeters) per year.

The Wabash River is the longest river in Indiana. The Wabash forms the southwestern border of the state. It then runs across the entire northern half of the state.

Indiana can have violent storms, especially in the spring. In 1974, at least 20 tornadoes hit throughout the state on the same day. The tornadoes killed 49 people and hurt more than 750 others.

Earthquakes are rare in Indiana but do sometimes happen. Indiana can also be affected by earthquakes that happen in neighboring states. Earthquakes in other states can cause damage to buildings in Indiana.

The cardinal is Indiana's state bird.

Indiana Bat

The Indiana bat is a shy and helpful animal. Each night, the bat eats more than its own weight in insects. In summer, the bats sleep during the day under the loose bark of dead trees. In winter, they fall into a deep sleep, or hibernate, in caves and mineshafts.

People sometimes disturb the caves in winter. They cut down the trees bats need for summer. During the last 15 years, more than half the bat population has disappeared from Indiana. The species is now considered endangered. State officials are taking steps to protect the bat and its territory.

Wildlife

Among the animals found in Indiana are deer, foxes, opossums, raccoons, and beaver. Endangered species include the bobcat, river otter, and the Indiana bat.

Indiana is home to many birds, including the cardinal, the state bird. Red-tailed hawks soar above Indiana. Several kinds of ducks live close to Indiana's lakes and rivers.

Visitors can see reconstructions of the village of Angel Mounds in Evansville.

Chapter 3

History of Indiana

Around 800 B.C., mound builders called the Adena people lived in Indiana. The Adena built large mounds of earth near rivers. Their tools, ornaments, and weapons have been found in the mounds. The mounds also served as burial grounds for the Adena people. Around 100 B.C., the Hopewell people built larger mounds.

Around A.D. 1000, the Mississippian people arrived in Indiana. They built a wall around a burial mound at a village called Angel Mounds. Angel Mounds was located where Evansville stands today. This village appears to have been the center of trade, government, and religion for the Mississippian people.

The Mississippians left no writing behind. No one knows exactly why Angel Mounds was deserted in 1450. Smaller Mississippian villages existed to the west of Angel Mounds as late as the 1600s. By the time the first Europeans reached Indiana, these villages were also deserted.

The Miami Indians moved into the area between 1100 and 1300. They hunted animals and grew corn and squash. Other tribes in Indiana were the Delaware, Shawnee, and Kickapoo. Most of these tribes came from regions outside of Indiana.

French Settlers

In 1679, René-Robert Cavelier, known as Sieur de La Salle, of France arrived in Indiana. He was traveling from Canada to the Mississippi River. In 1681, La Salle met with the Miami Indians in what is now Indiana.

La Salle claimed Indiana land in the name of France. By 1715, the French were trading blankets, beads, and other goods to the Indians for furs. In 1715, the French built Fort des Miamis at the Miami village of Kekionga. This village was near what is now Fort Wayne.

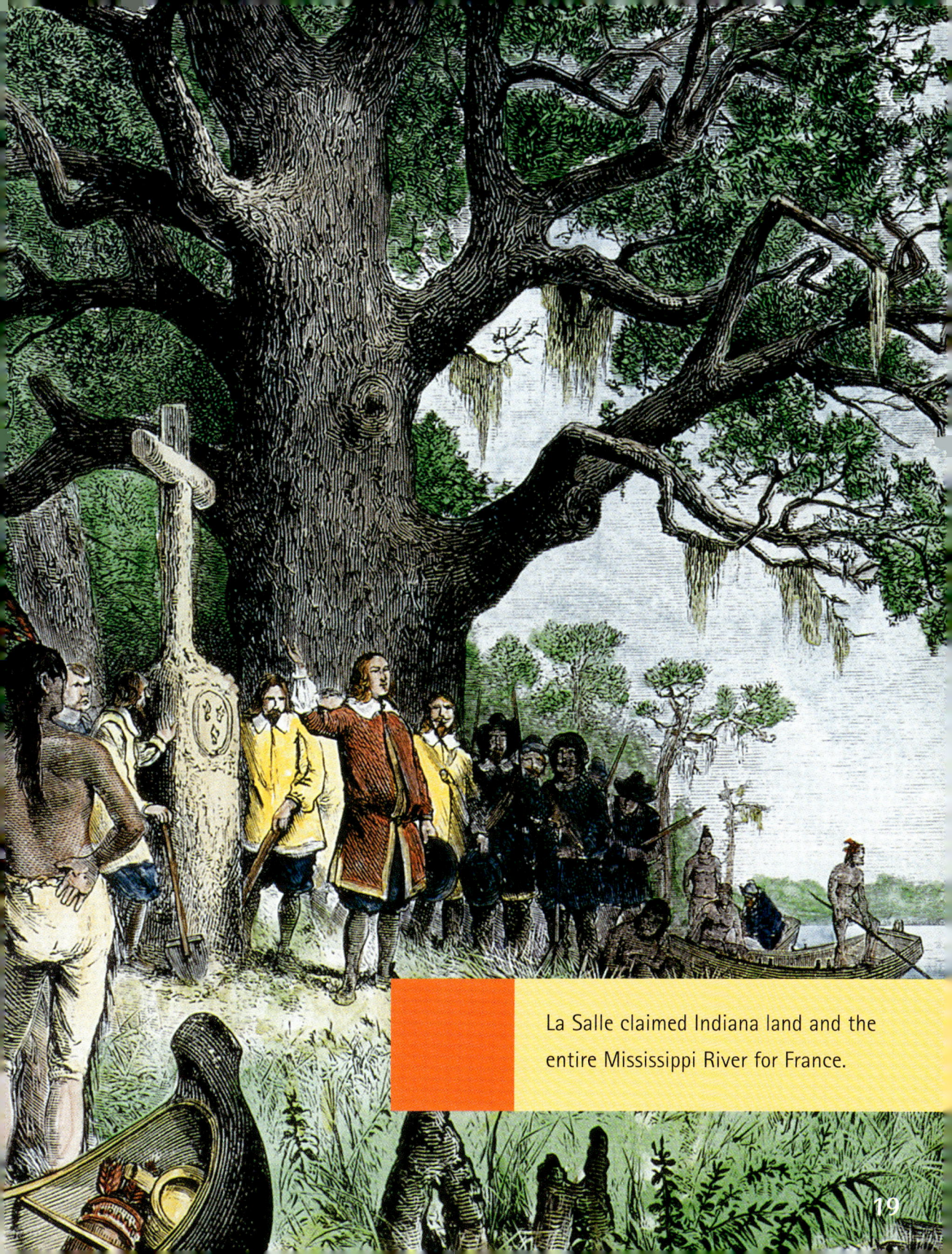

La Salle claimed Indiana land and the entire Mississippi River for France.

British Conflicts

Between 1754 and 1763, the British fought the French and Indian War. This war took place mostly to the east of Indiana, near the colonies. Great Britain won the war, and the claim to Indiana went to the British.

The 13 colonies rose against British rule in the Revolutionary War (1775–1783). The colonies created the United States of America. During that war, George Rogers Clark of Virginia led troops west to Illinois and Indiana. In 1779, Clark and his men captured Fort Sackville and Vincennes.

The Northwest Territory

After the war, the new U.S. Congress adopted the Northwest Ordinance. This law organized the land north and west of the Ohio River into the Northwest Territory. This land included Indiana. The ordinance also outlawed slavery in the region and gave American Indians certain land rights. Neither of these laws were closely followed.

By 1788, about 20,000 white settlers lived in the Northwest Territory. Most of them lived in Ohio. The American Indians feared that their lands would be taken by the settlers. They formed an army led by Miami Chief Little Turtle.

Little Turtle fought battles about land against the U.S. soldiers. In 1794, he lost to General "Mad Anthony" Wayne at the Battle of Fallen Timbers. The battle took place where Toledo, Ohio, stands today. General Wayne then marched to Fort des Miamis. He built a new fort on the other side of the river. He called it Fort Wayne.

Chief Little Turtle lost to General Wayne in the Battle of Fallen Timbers. Little Turtle fought to save his people's land.

In 1795, the Miami people signed a peace treaty with General Wayne. In 1827, most of the Miami left Indiana and moved to what is now Kansas.

Indiana Territory

In 1800, the Indiana Territory was created out of the Northwest Territory. This territory included areas that are now the states of Indiana, Michigan, Illinois, and Wisconsin. More than 5,000 new settlers lived there. William Henry Harrison was named governor, and Vincennes was the capital.

General Wayne defeated Chief Little Turtle and the Miami Indians at the Battle of Fallen Timbers.

Johnny Appleseed

Johnny Appleseed was born John Chapman in Massachusetts around 1775. At an early age, he decided to preserve nature and plant apple trees. He got leftover seeds from cider mills and planted trees wherever he went.

He lived simply, in harmony with nature and the American Indians. He sold or gave away his seeds and apple trees. He was famous for his kindness and his strength.

He lived near Fort Wayne from 1822 until his death in 1845. His grave marker is located in Johnny Appleseed Park in Fort Wayne. His cabin is preserved in a shopping mall. People have written many songs, stories, and poems about Johnny Appleseed.

By 1809, other territories had split from the Indiana Territory. The Indiana Territory shrunk to what is present-day Indiana.

American Indian Conflict

American Indians were unhappy that their land was being taken. Two Shawnee brothers gathered several tribes together. One of the brothers, Tecumseh, was known as the warrior. His brother, Tenskwatawa, was considered a religious leader. The two brothers tried to unite all American Indians. Tecumseh wanted to fight against settlers who tried to take away Indian land. In 1810, the brothers began attacking settlements.

In 1811, Governor Harrison and about 900 soldiers defeated Tenskwatawa's forces near the Tippecanoe and Wabash Rivers. Tecumseh took no part in the battle. The fight became known as the Battle of Tippecanoe. Harrison earned the nickname "Old Tippecanoe" by winning this battle.

Tecumseh and other American Indians attacked white settlements to defend their people's land.

Abraham Lincoln

By 1816, more than 60,000 settlers lived in Indiana. These settlers included the Lincoln family from Kentucky. Young Abraham Lincoln would later serve as U.S. president during the Civil War (1861–1865). In Indiana, Lincoln helped his father build a log cabin and plant crops. He also attended his first school in Indiana. The family moved to Illinois in 1830. Visitors can see Lincoln's boyhood home in Lincoln, Indiana.

Statehood

Indiana became the 19th state on December 11, 1816. Corydon in the southern part of the state was the first capital.

At that time, American Indians occupied more than two-thirds of the state. They lived mostly in the central and northern parts of the state. The state government began buying this land from the Indians.

In 1820, Indiana lawmakers decided to move the capital to the middle of the state. In 1825, Indianapolis was named the new state capital.

Early Advancements

Education is important to people in Indiana. Indiana's state constitution of 1816 was the first to call for free public schools open to all children. Many of Indiana's universities were founded in the mid-1800s.

Notre Dame is one of Indiana's most famous universities. It was founded in 1842. Notre Dame is known for the golden dome on the top of the Administration Building. Students of Notre Dame are called "Golden Domers."

Underground Railroad

In the mid-1800s, another kind of "railroad" was operating in Indiana. Thousands of slaves came through Indiana from the Southern states. The slaves were headed for Canada and freedom. Many Hoosiers helped them.

From 1826 to 1847, Levi and Catherine Coffin, of Fountain City, Indiana, hid more than 2,000 slaves. Southern slaveholders began to say that it seemed as if there was an Underground Railroad. They said that Levi Coffin was the railroad's president. Every slave Coffin helped reached freedom. Today, the Coffin house is a national historic landmark.

The first railroad line in Indiana was opened in 1847. It connected Indianapolis to Madison. Many railroad lines were built in the state in the 1850s.

Politics and the Civil War

In the early 1850s, the Republican Party was formed to oppose the spread of slavery. Indiana citizens supported anti-slavery laws. Hoosiers helped elect Republican Abraham Lincoln as president in 1860. Soon after, 11 Southern states left the United States. They formed the Confederate States of America. In April of 1861, the Confederacy attacked Fort Sumter in South Carolina, starting the Civil War (1861–1865).

Solving Injustices

In the late 1800s, the citizens of Indiana demanded that they receive fair treatment. After the Civil War, Indiana passed laws to allow African Americans to vote and hold office. Indiana women were allowed to go to the same colleges as men.

Many workers in Indiana's factories felt they were underpaid. Many felt they were made to work too many hours. Some felt they were mistreated by their bosses. Workers joined labor unions. These organizations fought for better pay and shorter work days. One of the earliest labor leaders was Eugene Debs of Terre Haute. Debs founded the American Railway Union. Labor laws were passed by Indiana lawmakers in 1879, 1893, and 1897. These laws improved working conditions.

World Wars and the Great Depression

More than 130,000 soldiers from Indiana served in World War I (1914–1918). At home, people in Indiana produced steel, food, and other goods for the military.

After World War I, the state's economy suffered. Jobs were hard to find. Many white men in Indiana joined the Ku Klux Klan (KKK). The group promoted hate against Catholics, Jews, African Americans, immigrants, and other groups. The KKK thought these people were evil. They also feared these people would take available jobs. The KKK set fires to homes and

Members of the KKK frightened and hurt African Americans, not only in Indiana, but all over the country.

businesses and hurt people that they hated. They also marched and wore masks in nighttime parades, trying to frighten people.

The head of the KKK in Indiana was David C. Stephenson. He called himself the Grand Dragon. He bribed many public officials, including Governor Ed Jackson and Indianapolis Mayor John Duvall.

Stephenson kidnapped and beat a woman. He refused to take her to a doctor, and she died. When he was arrested, Stephenson told the police the names of Klan members all over the state. He admitted to many illegal acts. In November 1925, Stephenson was sentenced to life in prison for murder.

The Indiana KKK membership stood at 178,000 members in 1924. By 1928, it had dropped to just 4,000 members. Today, very few people in Indiana belong to the Klan.

The Great Depression (1929–1939) was difficult for Indiana and the rest of the country. Many people lost their jobs and land. In 1937, Indiana suffered further when hundreds of people were killed in a flood in southern Indiana. The damage cost hundreds of millions of dollars.

The mills in Gary provided steel for the military in World War II.

World War II (1939–1945) boosted Indiana's economy. The war effort required steel, food, and other goods produced in Indiana. The war helped end the Great Depression.

Racial Equality

Many changes took place in Indiana and the rest of the country after World War II. Before 1949, African American and white students went to different schools. This forced separation of races is called segregation. In 1949, Indiana lawmakers made school segregation illegal. Whites and African Americans began to attend school together.

In 1967, Gary became the first major city in the United States to elect an African American mayor. Richard Hatcher was re-elected four times.

Indiana Today

Since 1980, more than 25 percent of Gary's people have moved away. Many Gary residents rely on the steel industry for jobs.

But steel manufacturing has declined. Jobs in Gary have become harder to find. Gary is now one of America's poorest cities.

Indiana faces many of the same problems other states have. Larger cities in Indiana have not been kept up well. The Indiana government raised taxes to make cities like Indianapolis look newer and more inviting for businesses and tourists.

The government is raising money to make cities like Indianapolis more attractive.

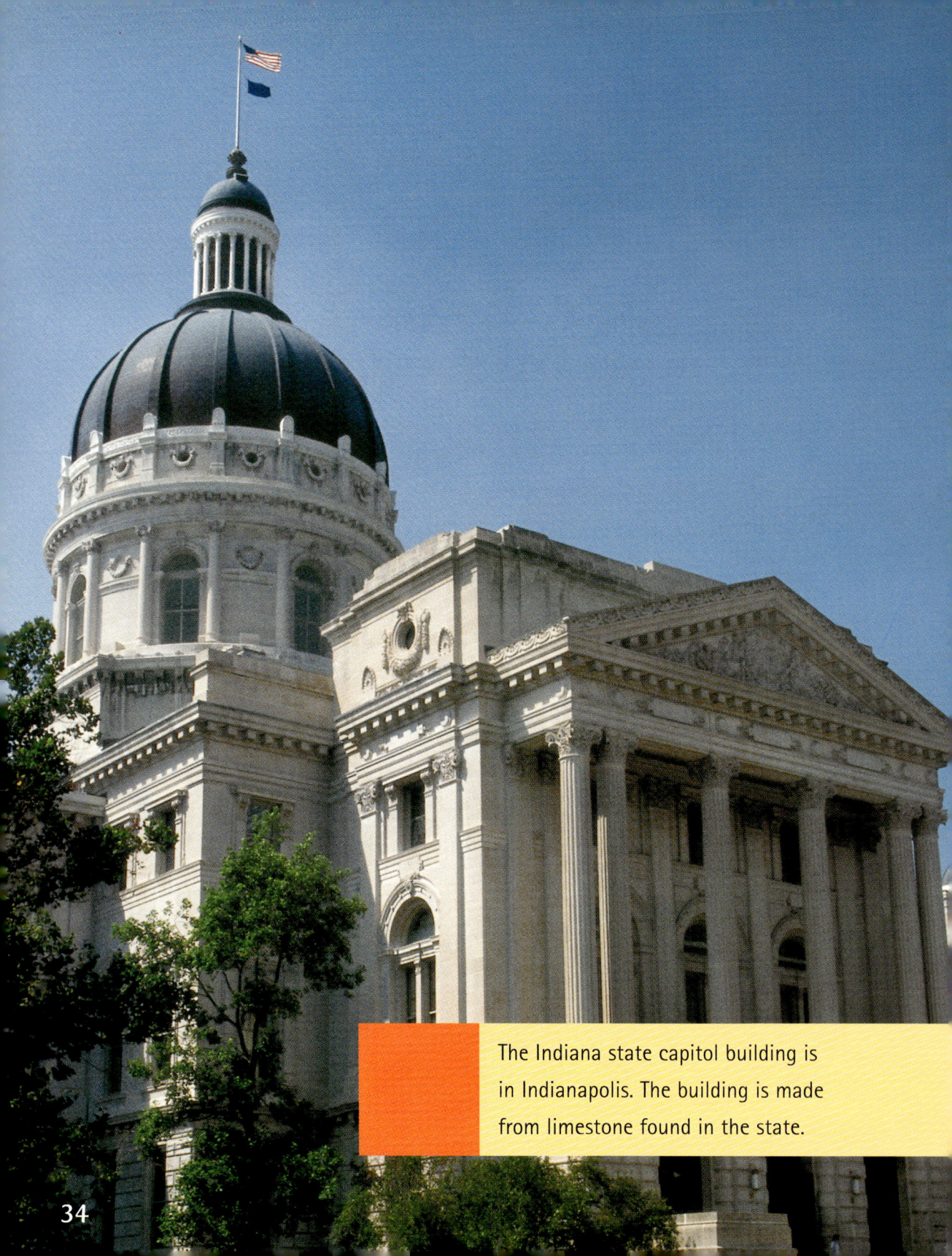

The Indiana state capitol building is in Indianapolis. The building is made from limestone found in the state.

Chapter 4

Government and Politics

Indiana's current constitution was adopted in 1851. It replaced an earlier one dating from 1816. The constitution of 1851 set up three branches of government. The executive branch carries out the laws. The legislative branch suggests laws and makes laws. The judicial branch interprets laws and tries court cases.

The governor heads the executive branch and is elected to a four-year term. He or she may not serve more than two terms in a row. The governor selects the heads of almost all state departments. He or she may reject, or veto, suggested laws.

The Indiana legislature is called the General Assembly. The General Assembly has a Senate with 50 members and a House of Representatives with 100 members. Senators and representatives suggest laws to benefit the public.

Indiana's Courts

The highest court in Indiana's judicial branch is the state supreme court. It has five judges. The court of appeals has 12 judges. If a person disagrees with a lower court ruling, the case can be retried in the court of appeals.

Judge nominees for these two courts are selected by a special commission. From this group, the governor selects the judges. Their two-year term is followed by an election. If the voters approve, the judges can serve for 10 more years.

Most Hoosier State counties have their own circuit courts. Some counties share courts. Circuit courts hear local cases. Many of these cases are about family issues such as child support and visitation rights. Circuit court judges are elected to six-year terms.

Indiana's State Government

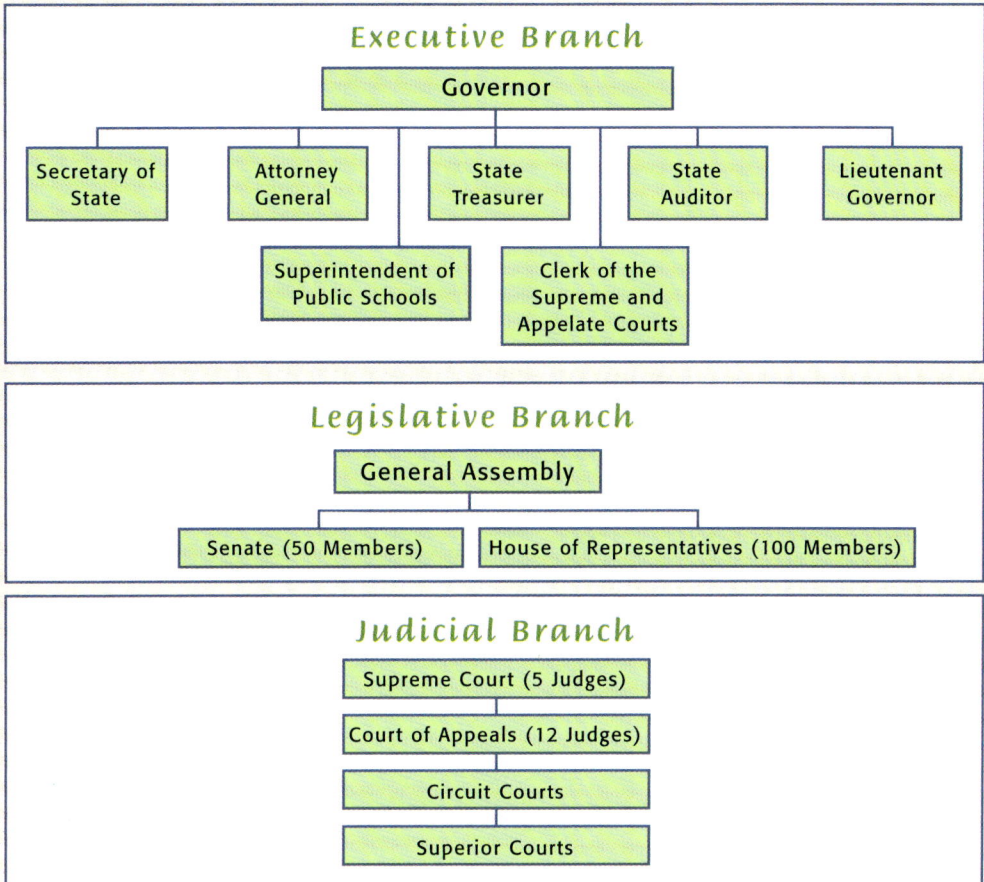

Executive Branch

Governor

- Secretary of State
- Attorney General
- State Treasurer
- State Auditor
- Lieutenant Governor
- Superintendent of Public Schools
- Clerk of the Supreme and Appelate Courts

Legislative Branch

General Assembly

- Senate (50 Members)
- House of Representatives (100 Members)

Judicial Branch

- Supreme Court (5 Judges)
- Court of Appeals (12 Judges)
- Circuit Courts
- Superior Courts

Some counties also have superior courts. Some counties have juvenile courts, probate courts, and criminal courts. All of the judges in these courts are elected to four-year terms. City courts, town courts, and a county court system also make up the Indiana court system.

Benjamin Harrison

Benjamin Harrison of Indianapolis was the grandson of William Henry Harrison, the first governor of the Indiana Territory. In 1888, Benjamin was elected the 23rd president of the United States. He lived in Indianapolis and fought in the Civil War.

After the war, he became a Republican Senator. He worked for the rights of American Indians, war heroes, and farmers. Benjamin helped pass the Sherman Anti-Trust Act. This act helped farmers and small businesses by outlawing larger businesses completely controlling an industry. These large businesses were called monopolies.

In 1892, after losing re-election, he returned to Indianapolis to practice law and write. He became famous in international law. Today, his home is a national historic landmark and a popular tourist spot.

Local Government

Most of Indiana's 92 counties are headed by a board of county commissioners. Other county officials include the auditor,

treasurer, recorder, surveyor, sheriff, coroner, and assessor. All of these positions are four-year terms.

Most Indiana cities have the mayor and council form of government. Boards of trustees govern towns. A township trustee and township advisory board governs each township. The members of city councils, boards of trustees, and advisory boards are all elected to office.

National Government and Politics

Like all states, Indiana has two U.S. senators. It sends 10 representatives to the House of Representatives in Washington, D.C. These people represent Indiana's ideas and opinions in the federal government. Indiana tends to be more conservative. Indiana traditionally votes Republican in national elections.

Farming is still an important part of Indiana's economy. Indiana is one of the largest producers of corn.

Chapter 5

Economy and Resources

Agriculture was the center of Indiana's economy until the early 1900s. Rich farmland was left behind when forests were cut down. In 1832, work began on the Wabash and Erie Canal. The canal helped Indiana farmers ship their crops to market.

The Great Depression of the 1930s was difficult for farmers. Prices for crops fell, and many farmers lost their land. After World War II, the number of farms and farm workers declined. Now, about two-thirds of the land in the state is used for farming.

Farming is still important to Indiana's economy. Soybeans, corn, wheat, and oats are the most important crops in the state. Tomatoes, strawberries, melons, and popcorn are grown in the southwestern part of the state. Indiana is the second largest producer of popcorn in the country. Popcorn manufacturer Orville Redenbacher grew up in Indiana.

Farmers in Indiana also raise cattle, poultry, and hogs. Indiana ranks sixth in the country in hog production. There are more than three million hogs in the state.

Industry and Natural Resources

The state's industries grew after the Civil War, and many small factories were built. Mining for coal and limestone increased. In 1886, natural gas was discovered in central Indiana. But the gas was used wastefully, and within 15 years it was nearly gone.

In 1906, the United States Steel Corporation put its largest mill in the Calumet region of northwestern Indiana. The mill created the city of Gary. The city was named after its chairperson, Elbert Gary. By 1920, the Calumet region was one of the leading industrial centers in North America.

Indiana is the nation's sixth largest producer of hogs. Pork sandwiches are famous in Indiana.

Auto Industry

Indiana became a big auto-making center in the early 1900s. One of the first gasoline-powered cars in America, the Haynes Pioneer, was made in Kokomo in 1894. In 1902, the Studebaker brothers began making cars in South Bend. Many other factories in the state began making car parts. After the 1920s, auto manufacturing declined in the state. Making parts for cars is still a part of Indiana's economy.

After World War I, prices for manufactured goods fell. Gary's mills almost shut down completely. One-fourth of the state's workers lost their jobs. The flood of 1937 cost the state hundreds of millions of dollars, further hurting the economy. World War II helped end the Great Depression.

Today, industry is growing in Indiana. Indiana is one of the most industrialized states in the country. The state has more than 11,000 factories. These factories make iron, steel, food products, wood products, chemicals, and medicine. Indiana is the largest steel manufacturer in the country. Eli Lilly and Company is a major medicine company that has its headquarters in Indianapolis. Lumber is also important. The Hoosier State is the third-leading state in the country in hardwood lumber production.

Lumber is stacked in lumber yards before being transported to markets to be sold.

THANKS!

The Herald-Times • Hoosier Times

THANKS!

#1 FAN
INDIANA

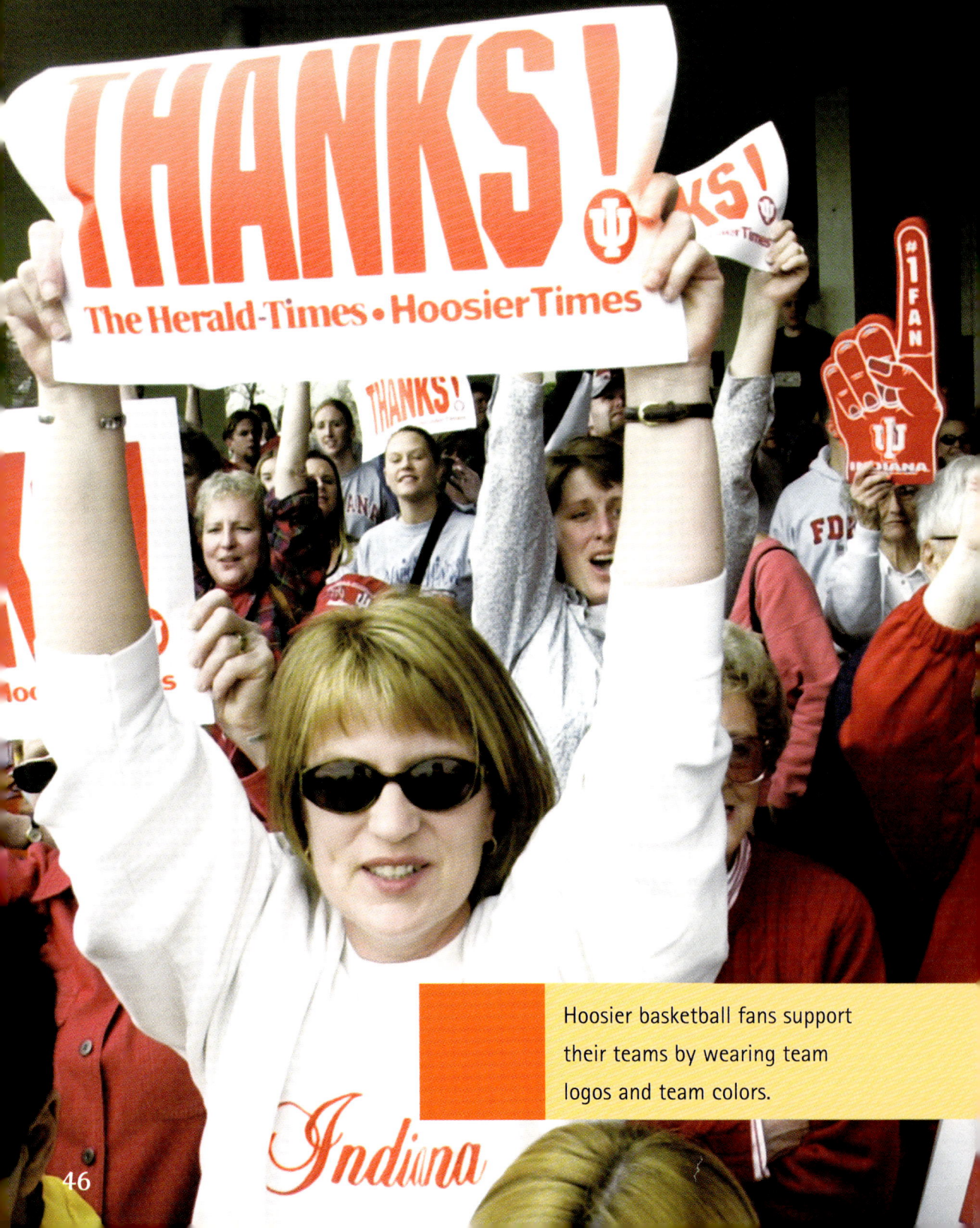

Hoosier basketball fans support their teams by wearing team logos and team colors.

Indiana

Chapter 6

People and Culture

Indianapolis is home to many sports fans and teams. The Indiana Pacers pro basketball team plays in Indianapolis. The state high school basketball tournament is also held in Indianapolis every spring. The NFL Colts also play in Indianapolis. Car racing fans from all over the country watch the Indy 500 every Memorial Day weekend.

Hoosiers are very serious about their basketball. Gymnasiums in Indiana high schools are known to be some of the biggest in the country. In 2002, Indianapolis hosted the World Basketball Championship. Players from many nations took part in the championship. Indiana also has a professional women's basketball team called Indiana Fever.

The Indiana Basketball Hall of Fame is located in New Castle. There, the history of basketball in Indiana is recorded and preserved. Thousands of Hoosiers and tourists visit the museum every year.

Hoosiers

Indiana's population is mostly white. The majority of Hoosiers have European backgrounds. Many early immigrants were Irish and German. In the late 1800s and early 1900s, many people from eastern European countries like Russia and Poland came to Indiana. Many of them worked in the steel

The Amish use horses and buggies for transportation.

Indiana's Ethnic Background

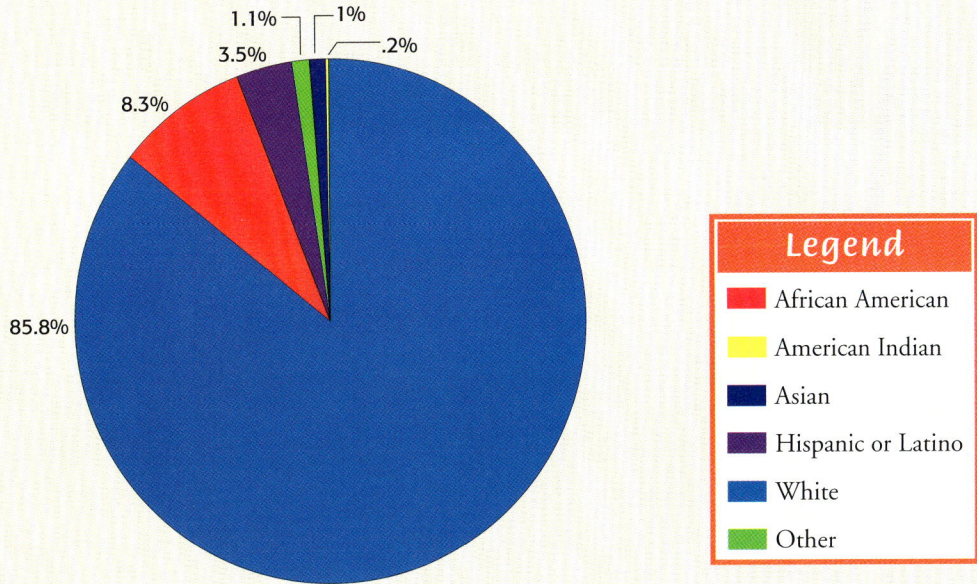

1.1%
3.5%
8.3%
85.8%
1%
.2%

Legend
- African American
- American Indian
- Asian
- Hispanic or Latino
- White
- Other

mills of Gary. African Americans also worked there. Gary and Indianapolis still have the largest populations of African Americans in the state. Large populations of Hispanic Americans live in Indianapolis, Hammond, and East Chicago.

The Amish came to northern Indiana in the late 1830s. This religious group settled near Nappanee, which became famous for wood products. Amish cabinets and furniture are still prized by antique dealers. Today, the Amish live much as they did in the 1800s. They do not use electricity. They use horses instead of cars and tractors.

History and the Arts

Preserving history and art is very important to Indiana's people. Indiana has many museums and historical sites to visit. Fishers is the home of Conner Prairie. Visitors to this living history site can see how pioneers lived in the 1830s. Costumed guides tell the details of frontier life.

Vincennes in southern Indiana is one of the oldest towns in the state. It is the home of the George Rogers Clark Memorial. The memorial honors his work during the Revolutionary War.

Evansville is home to many historic places and monuments. Angel Mounds shows reconstructions of what life was like for American Indians around 1250. The Four Freedoms Monument stands in Evansville. This monument has four pillars that represent the freedoms enjoyed by U.S. citizens. Evansville is also the home of the Germania Maennerchor Volksfest. This festival includes food and music that celebrate German culture. Visitors can learn about the World War II Evansville shipyard at the Evansville Museum of Arts, History, and Science. The museum also has art shows and a planetarium.

The Four Freedoms Monument is located in Evansville. The monument opened in 1976 to celebrate the U.S. Bicentennial. The four pillars represent the freedom of speech, the freedom of religion, the freedom from fear, and the freedom from oppression.

The Children's Museum of Indianapolis is the largest children's museum in the world. It has the world's biggest model train collection.

Columbus is called the Architectural Showplace of America. Many famous modern architects have designed

The Ameritech Switching Station is an example of the modern architecture in Columbus.

Santa Claus, Indiana

Northeast of Evansville is the town of Santa Claus. The town was named on Christmas in 1846. In 1946, a theme park called Santa Claus Land was built. In 1984, the park's name was changed to Holiday World. The park has rides, toy and doll museums, and a Santa for visitors to meet. Each year, thousands of letters from children come to Santa Claus, Indiana.

unique buildings here. A colorful elementary school, made up of many small buildings connected by tube-shaped ramps, is located in Columbus.

The people of Indiana are loyal to their state and their country. They also are hardworking. Hoosiers have given much to the country in times of need. Hoosiers take pride in the accomplishments of their state and their country.

Recipe: Honey Baked Apples

Johnny Appleseed lived in Indiana and planted many apple trees there. Indiana is home to more than 50 apple orchards.

Ingredients

4 apples
4 tablespoons (60 mL) honey
½ cup (120 mL) seedless raisins
1 cup (240 mL) apple juice or
  cider
4 teaspoons (20 mL) ground
  cinnamon

Equipment

knife or apple corer
oven-safe glass dish with a cover
measuring cups
measuring spoons
potholders
basting brush

What You Do

1. Preheat oven to 400°F (200°C).

2. Wash the apples.

3. With a knife or apple corer, cut out the center of each apple to remove the core. Do not cut all the way through the apple. The apple should have a hole in the top but not the bottom.

4. Place the apples in the glass dish.

5. Pour one tablespoon (15 mL) of honey into the cored-out center of each apple.

6. Fill the centers of each apple with raisins.

7. Pour the apple juice or cider over each apple.

8. Sprinkle cinnamon on top of each apple.

9. Put the cover on the dish.

10. Place the dish in the oven and bake 45 minutes, or until apples are soft.

11. Remove dish from the oven.

12. Baste apples with the sauce at the bottom of the dish.

Makes 4 servings

Indiana's Flag and Seal

Indiana's Flag

Indiana's state flag is blue with 19 gold stars around a flaming gold torch. The stars symbolize Indiana's position as the 19th state. The word "Indiana" is lettered in gold above the largest star, which represents the state. Thirteen of the stars are arranged in an outer circle to represent the original 13 colonies. The flag was designed by Paul Hadley of Moorseville, Indiana. It was adopted in 1917.

Indiana's State Seal

Indiana's state seal was adopted in 1963, but it was used as early as 1801. The seal features a woodsman chopping down a tree while a buffalo jumps over a log. Around the outside of the seal, the year of statehood appears along with the words "Seal of the State of Indiana."

Almanac

General Facts

Nickname: Hoosier State

Population: 6,080,485 (U.S. Census 2000)
Population rank: 14th

Capital: Indianapolis

Largest cities: Indianapolis, Fort Wayne, Evansville, South Bend, Gary

Agriculture

Agricultural products: Corn, popcorn, wheat, oats, soybeans, hogs

Climate

Average summer temperature: 73 degrees Fahrenheit (23 degrees Celsius)

Average winter temperature: 30 degrees Fahrenheit (minus 1 degree Celsius)

Average annual precipitation: 40.5 inches (103 centimeters)

Geography

Area: 35,870 square miles (92,903 square kilometers)
Size rank: 38th

Highest point: Hoosier Hill in Wayne County 1,257 feet (383 meters) above sea level

Lowest point: Posey County, 320 feet (97.5 meters) above sea level

Peony

Bird: Cardinal

Flower: Peony

Motto: The Crossroads of America

Poem: "Indiana," by Arthur Franklin Mapes

Rock: Limestone

Song: "On the Banks of the Wabash, Far Away," written and composed by Paul Dresser

Tree: Tulip tree (yellow poplar)

Industries: Steel, auto parts, and agriculture

Natural resources: Limestone, coal, hardwoods

First governor: Jonathan Jennings

Statehood: December 11, 1816 (19th state)

U.S. Representatives: 10

U.S. Senators: 2

U.S. electoral votes: 12

Counties: 92

Cardinal

57

Timeline

State History

1000–1450
Mississippian people live at the village of Angel Mounds.

1763
Great Britain claims the Indiana region after winning the French and Indian War.

1679
La Salle claims the Indiana region for France.

1794
General Anthony Wayne defeats Little Turtle and the Miami people; founds Fort Wayne.

1800
The Indiana territory is created. Vincennes is the capital.

1811
William Henry Harrison defeats Tenskwatawa's forces at the Battle of Tippecanoe.

U.S. History

1620
Pilgrims settle in North America.

1775–1783
Great Britain and the American colonies fight the Revolutionary War.

1812–1814
Great Britain and the United States fight the War of 1812.

1816

Indiana becomes the 19th state. Young Abraham Lincoln and his family move to Indiana, where they will live until 1830.

1937

A flood kills hundreds of Hoosiers.

Greetings from INDIANA
2002 USA 34

1967

Richard Hatcher of Gary becomes the first African American mayor of a major city.

1906

The U.S. Steel Corporation creates the city of Gary and puts its largest steel mill there.

1964

U.S. Congress passes the Civil Rights Act.

1914–1918

World War I is fought. The United States enters the war in 1917.

1939–1945

World War II is fought. The United States enters the war in 1941.

1861–1865

The Northern and Southern states fight the Civil War.

1929–1939

The United States experiences the Great Depression.

2001

Terrorists attack the World Trade Center and the Pentagon.

Words to Know

Amish (AH-mish)—a religious group of people who do not use electric machinery

Confederacy (kuhn-FED-ur-uh-see)—the 11 states that left the United States during the Civil War

glacier (GLAY-shur)—large sheet of moving ice

hibernate (HYE-bur-nate)—to fall into a deep sleep

Ku Klux Klan (KOO KLUHX KLHAN)—a group that promoted hate against Catholics, Jews, African Americans, immigrants, and other groups

monopoly (muh-NOP-uh-lee)—a large company that has complete control over an industry

segregation (seg-ruh-GAY-shuhn)—to separate people of different races

veto (VEE-toh)—to reject a law

To Learn More

Boekhoff, P.M., and Kallen, Stuart A. *Indiana*. Seeds of a Nation. San Diego: Kidhaven Press, 2002.

Gregson, Susan R. *Tecumseh: Shawnee Leader*. Let Freedom Ring. Mankato, Minn: Bridgestone Books, 2003

Ling, Bettina. *Indiana*. From Sea to Shining Sea. New York: Children's Press, 2003.

Swain, Gwenyth. *Indiana*. Hello U.S.A. Minneapolis: Lerner Publications, 2002.

Internet Sites

Track down many sites about Indiana.
Visit the FACT HOUND at http://www.facthound.com

IT IS EASY! IT IS FUN!
1) Go to *http://www.facthound.com*
2) Type in: 0736815821
3) Click on "FETCH IT" and
   FACT HOUND will find several
   links hand-picked by our editors.

Relax and let our pal FACT HOUND do the research for you!

Places to Write and Visit

Angel Mounds
8215 Pollack Avenue
Evansville, IN 47715

Conner Prairie Living History Museum
13400 Allisonville Road
Fishers, IN 46038-4499

Indiana Historical Society
450 West Ohio Street
Indianapolis, IN 46202

Indiana Tourism Division
One North Capitol
Suite 700
Indianapolis, IN 46204-2288

Office of the Governor
State House
Room 206
Indianapolis, IN 46204-2797

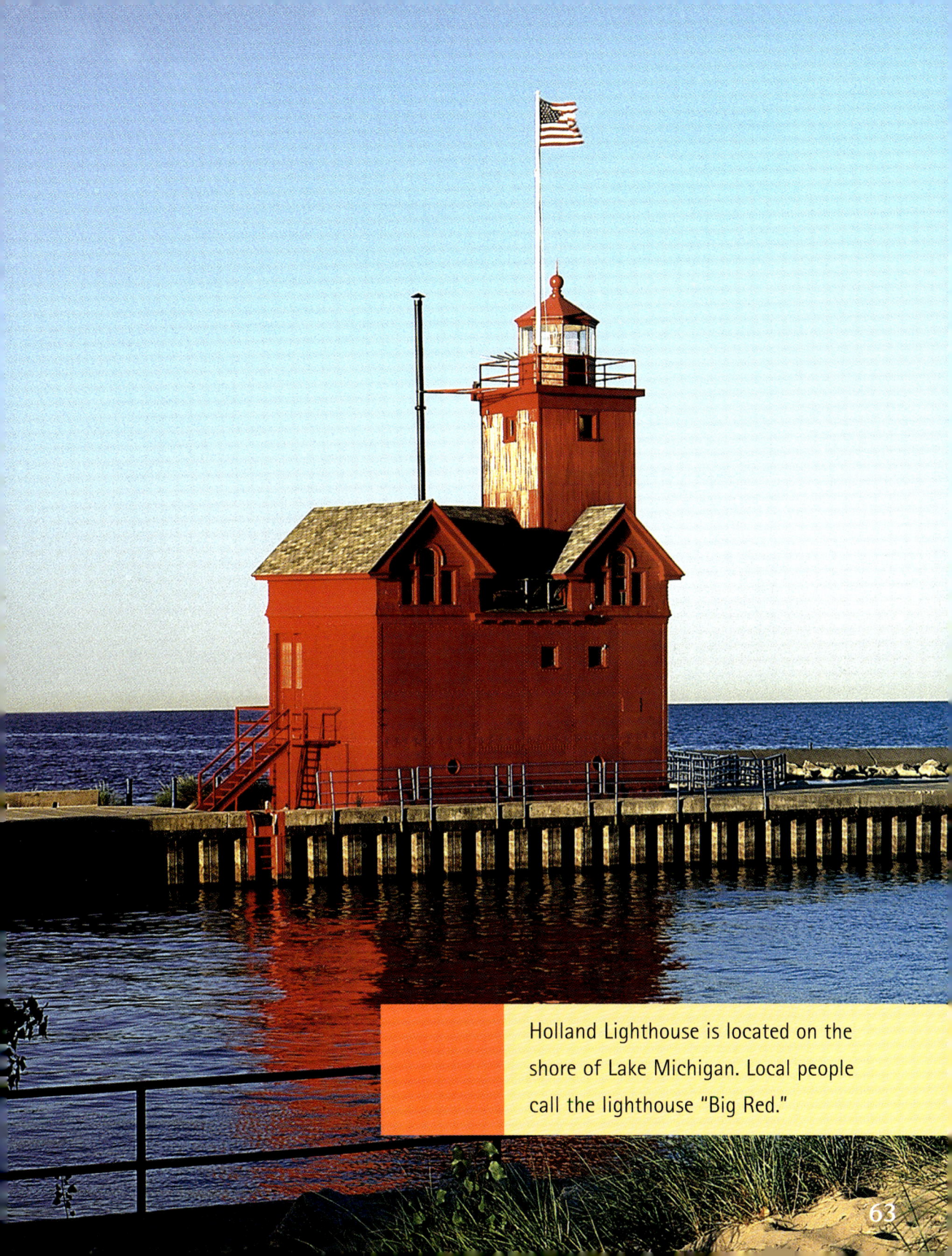

Holland Lighthouse is located on the shore of Lake Michigan. Local people call the lighthouse "Big Red."

Index

Adena people, 17
African Americans, 28, 29,
    31–32, 49
American Indians, 18,
    20–22, 23–24, 25, 38,
    51
Amish, 48, 49
Angel Mounds, 16, 17–18,
    51
Appleseed, Johnny, 23

basketball, 46, 47–48

caves, 10, 15
Children's Museum, 52
Civil War, 25, 27–28, 38,
    43
Clark, George Rogers, 20,
    50
climate, 13–14
Coffin, Levi, 27
Columbus, 52–53
Confederacy, 28
Conner Prairie, 50
Corydon, 25
crops, 10, 25, 40, 41, 42

economy, 29, 31, 40, 41–45
education, 26, 31–32
Evansville, 16, 17, 51, 53
executive branch, 35

Fallen Timbers, Battle of,
    21, 22
farming, 8, 9, 10, 40,
    41–42
flood, 30, 44
Fort des Miamis, 18, 21
Fort Wayne, 18, 21, 23
Four Freedoms Monument,
    51
French and Indian War, 20

furniture, 10, 49

Gary, 31, 32–33, 43, 44, 49
glaciers, 9
government, 25, 33, 35–39
Great Depression, 30–31,
    41, 44

Harrison, Benjamin, 38
Harrison, William Henry,
    22, 24, 38
Hispanic Americans, 49
hogs, 42, 43
Holiday World, 53
Hopewell people, 17

immigrants, 29, 48
Indiana Basketball Hall of
    Fame, 48
Indiana bat, 15
Indiana Territory, 22–23, 38
Indianapolis, 4, 5, 6, 26,
    27, 30, 33, 34, 38, 45,
    47, 49, 52
Indianapolis 500, 5–6, 47
industry, 32, 38, 43–45

judicial branch, 35, 36–37

Ku Klux Klan, 29–30

labor unions, 28
Lake Michigan, 6, 63
La Salle, René-Robert
    Cavelier, 18, 19
legislative branch, 35, 36
limestone, 34, 43
Lincoln, Abraham, 25, 28
Little Turtle, Chief, 21, 22
lumber, 45

Mississippian people, 17–18

museums, 50–52, 53
natural resources, 43
Northwest Territory, 20–22
Notre Dame, 26

politics, 27–28, 39
population, 21, 22, 25, 32,
    48–49

railroad, 27
Republican, 27–28, 38, 39
Revolutionary War, 20, 50

Santa Claus, 53
segregation, 32
slavery, 20, 27–28
state flag, 55
statehood, 25
state seal, 55
steel, 29, 31, 32–33, 45,
    48–49
Stephenson, David C., 30

Tecumseh, 24
Tenskwatawa, 24
Tippecanoe, Battle of, 24
tourism, 10, 33, 38, 48,
    50–51
trees, 10, 15, 23

Underground Railroad, 27

Vincennes, 20, 22, 50

Wabash River, 12, 13, 24
Wayne, General Anthony,
    21–22
wildlife, 15
World War I, 29, 44
World War II, 31, 41, 44,
    51

West Union School
23870 NW West Union Road
Hillsboro, Oregon 97124